Tickle Me, Don't Tickle Me

Tickle Me, Don't Tickle Me

And Other Poems for Magnificent, Turbo-Loaded, Triple-Charged Children

JERRY PINTO

Illustrated by Sunaina Coelho

An Imprint of Speaking Tiger

TALKING CUB
Speaking Tiger Books L.L.P
4381/4, Ansari Road, Daryaganj
New Delhi 110002

Published in paperback in Talking Cub by Speaking Tiger
Book in 2019

Text copyright © Jerry Pinto 2019
Illustrations © Sunaina Coelho 2019

ISBN: 978-93-89231-57-1
eISBN: 978-93-89231-56-4

10 9 8 7 6 5 4 3 2 1

The moral right of the author has been asserted.

No part of this publication may be reproduced, transmitted, or stored in a retrieval system, in any form or by any means, electronic, mechanical, photocopying, recording or otherwise, without the prior permission of the publisher.

This book is sold subject to the condition that it shall not, by way of trade or otherwise, be lent, resold, hired out, or otherwise circulated, without the publisher's prior consent, in any form of binding or cover other than that in which it is published.

Contents

Tick Tock Tock	7
Can You?	8
I Could Be Your Friend if…	9
In Bed	10
Formula for a Funny Poem	11
We Need New Days of the Week	12
Clean Up Your Act, Sol!	13
This Is What Happens to Children Who Dig Their Noses in Public	14
This Is What Happens to Children Who Scratch (Ick) in Public	17
What Happens to the Kids Who Won't Sit Down When the Parade Begins and Thus Block the View of Someone in Front of Them	20
What Happens to Children Who Say They Are Going to Fail Their Exams but Then Stand First	22
This Is What Happens to Children Who Scream in Public	28
This Is What Happens to Children Who Boast Incessantly	29
Camels	34
Bats	35
Sad	36
Happy	37
Seasons	38
A Questoon	39
Loop D'Whoop and Champ	40
Cootie at the Baker's	47

History (in brief)	48
True Story	49
In Defence of Rudy	51
Zoo Announcement	53
The Hamster	55
Question	56
Hungry in Mathematics Class	57
A Mathematical Love Story	58
My Cat	60
Our Puppy	61
Which Puppy?	62
Puppy Licks	63
More Ink!	64
Sellin' a Melon	66
Kiwi, Kiwi, Kiwikiwi	67
I'd Rather Read	68
Peppy of the Steppe	70
Stubby Joe	76
Tickle Me, Don't Tickle Me	77
Breakfast Rhymes	78
Reading	80
Girly	81
Hair-oil Horror	82
Advice to Mothers	84
There's a Monster in My Garden	85
They Took Papa Away in a Car	86
Whatever the Weather	88
When the Music Starts	90
When the Music Stops	91
What Do You Want to Be When You Grow Up?	92

Tick Tock Tock

Tick tock tock
In the night.

Tick tock tock
Out of sight.

Tick tock tock
Is it an echo?

Tick tock tock
Oh, it's a gecko.

Can You?

Can you squeak?
Can you creak?
Can you howl?
Can you growl?
Can you groan?
Can you drone?
Can you sputter?
Can you mutter?
Can you rumble?
Can you mumble?
Can you beep?
Can you cheep?
Can you hiss?
Like thissssssssssssssssssssssssssssssss...

I Could Be Your Friend if...

I could be your friend if you weren't so tall;
If you'd promise to catch me whenever I fall;
If you'd just let me play with your bouncy new ball.

I could be your friend if you only looked better;
If you had a dog like a European setter;
If only you were a better go-getter.

I could be your friend if you only ran faster;
If your ray gun were really a neutrino blaster;
If your face weren't in such a state of disaster.

This isn't a test, it's an exam;
Pass it and we'll be butter and jam,
But *you'll* have to take me just as I am.

In Bed

I was lying in my bed
When I wrote a poem in my head.
I said it aloud, I said it twice
I thought it sounded rather nice.
I went to sleep and in the morn
What poem? It had simply g o n e.

Moral: Don't write things down in your head.
Keep pen and paper by your bed.

Formula for a Funny Poem

Oh   dit dit da dit dit   eagle

It   dit dit da dit dit   regal

But   dit dit da dit dit   beagle

If   dit dit da dit dit   legal

We Need New Days of the Week

Monday, I'm grumpy because I didn't sleep.
Tuesday, the weekend's so far I could weep.
Wednesday's a word that's tough to get right.
Thursday—at least the weekend's in sight.
Friday, who cares? It's just about waiting.
Satursunday zips by, it's simply deflating.

So we need some new days
Like a Me-day.
I'd want Me-day every day.
But okay, let's have it in the middle of the week.
And since I'm nice and have a gentle streak,
We can have a You-day.
Maybe tomorrow, because today
Is Me-day.
Whee-day!

Clean Up Your Act, Sol!

A year should have 360 days

Thataways

Each month could have 30 days

Thataways

Each week could have five days

Thataways

Each week we'd have three school days

See?

Now someone go tell the sun

To mend his ways.

Do I have to do all the work around here?

This Is What Happens to Children Who Dig Their Noses in Public

Here is a most interesting case,
Note the expression on his face.
His eyes are bulging, lips askew
He must be feeling something new.

When he lived his name was Jose
He regularly dug his nose.
Every moment he could spare
He spent with finger inside nare.

He was a connoisseur of snot
Wet or dry, it mattered not.
When a lump had been extracted
His attention got contracted

He studied it with intensity
Measured its weight and density;
Rolled it up, stretched it out:
All that slithered from his snout.

But one day when in hot pursuit,
Of something deep within his snoot,
A slippery, slithery little gob
That kept sliding up his knob,

Delving deep and delving strong
Jose's finger got it wrong.
Broke through nose and hit the brain;
He'd never be the same again.

When they found him, he was rigid,
For that nose-exploring digit
Had broken through the pia mater
And the fatter, dura mater.

This caused his brain to spring a leak
And before the boy could squeak
His brain poured out as through a nozzle
Through that much-abused schnozzle.

Jose would not have died in vain
(No one knows if he felt pain)
If you will please heed this warning
Dig just once and in the morning.

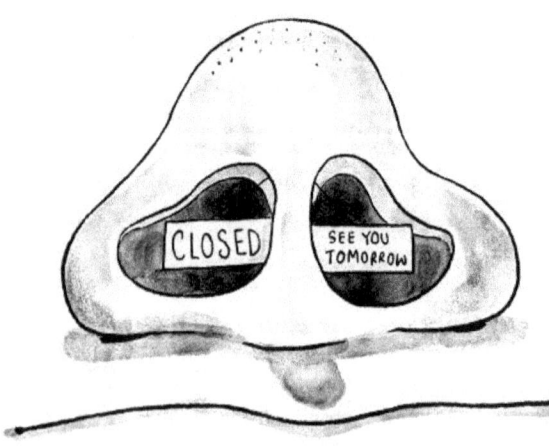

This Is What Happens to Children Who Scratch (Ick) in Public

Cross my heart and hope to die
Chuck's not scratched inside his eye
But every other bit of skin
He's scratched enough to make it thin
And red and raw and sticky-looking.
So Chuck was somewhat icky-looking.
His father had Chuck's nails cut short
But Chuck promptly went out and bought
A foot-long ruler made of beech
That enabled him to reach
All those distant bits of back,
That has been safe from all attack.

His mother screamed, his father snorted.
But Chuck the scratcher just retorted,
'I do no harm to no one else
And as for scars, I like my welts.'

Friends suggest a change of scene:
'Surround the boy with lots of green.'
'Keep calamine in easy reach.'
'Take the lad off to the beach.'
And since the last suggestion came
With free housing, Chuck's parents were game.

Off they jauntered to the beach
With their spawn in easy reach.
Did it change things? Here's the catch
Chuck continued scratch-scratch.
Yes, even when Chuck was swimming
His nails would o'er his skin be skimming.

But skin that has been scritched and scratched
Can soon begin to get detached.
This now happened to icky Chuck
The boy was running out of luck.
For when your skin starts to secede,
Blood vessels notice; and they bleed.
This is okay in the park
Where you never find a shark

Near the slide or see-saw area;
But in the sea? Nothing's scarier
Than a fish that's always willing
To do some headline-making killing;
A fish in whom a drop of blood
Can start a fully drooly flood.

Silver-quick, the big
shark slurped
Chuck up and then it
burped
And wandered off
again to search
For the next course—
a dozing perch?
So *if* you scratch more
than you oughter
Just don't do it in the water.

What Happens to the Kids Who Won't Sit Down When the Parade Begins and Thus Block the View of Someone in Front of Them

In every small-town parade,
And 'every' is true, I'm afraid,
There is a little man or maid
Who thinks they are glass-fact'ry made.

They'll stand up when the road is bare.
They'll stand up and look at empty air.
They'll stand up though they have a chair.
They'll stand up as if only they were there.

This year I went to see a show
Not very distant from Jaipore.
I thought I had a first-row seat.
(Since I am short, that is a treat.)

But when the band began to play,
With not a second of delay,
A little boy began to bray,
And wandered right into my way.

I held my tongue; I kept my peace.
I wished to shoot him in the knees.
I didn't for no good comes to these
Who do such things because they tease.

And I was right. When we had sung
The anthem and the bells were rung,
An elephant unloosed his bung
And covered up the boy with dung.

So little kids, now here's the law,
Beseat yourselves, feet on the floor.
Or you might ask for something raw
Right from an elephant's backdoor.

What Happens to Children Who Say They Are Going to Fail Their Exams but Then Stand First

The exams are coming,
My head is humming,
With things I just didn't mug,
But the girl who stands first,
Has a tearful outburst:
'Oh man! I'm sure to plug.'

The tests draw near,
Once more I fear,
The red marks on my report,
But the girl who stands first
(For her red blood I thirst)
Declares she'll score a zot.

When the reports are posted,
And my backside is toasted,
Once more she will declare,
'It's just sheer luck
That I didn't duck'
Though her ranking is clearly up there.

This lugubrious twit,
Would worry a bit,
If she heard the tale of Zenobia,
A lady who claimed,
Her brain had been maimed,
By examination phobia.

Zinny, need I say
Never could play
Since she was so busy with mugging
But when a test neared
She was always a-feared
That she was going to be plugging.

Each final exam!
The same old scam,
Dear Zinny was sure to moot.
Until one year,
The demons, I fear,
Decided to give her the boot.

The teacher was old
I could make so bold
To say she had nary a clue.
With a half-tired air,
She climbed to her chair
And stuck to it, soldered with glue.

The paper fell
(It rang a death knell)
Upon every tremulous table.
All the kids' heads went down
There was fear all around
This is the fabric of fable.

Q1 is a zonker!
Q2 is a conker!
Q3's a hard nut to crack.
As for Q4
I simply don't know.
This paper will fracture your back.

Then through the hall
Came a furious bawl,
A scream of dreadful surprise
It was Zinny shrieking
Like a demon squeaking
At a djinn extracting its eyes.

Zinny's here, Zinny's there
Zinny's under her chair
She's screaming as loud as a banshee
There's froth at her mouth
Her mind's going south
For Zinny can never fail, can she?

The old teacher's calls
They ring down the halls
As she gets help for Zenobia
The doctors look grave
'There's no chance to save
The cortico-spasmoidal lobe, here.'

Ten minutes after
We're all going dafter
Trying to sort out the mess
A teacher announces
With suitable flounces
'Children, now here's a stop press.

'Now kids of Class 6,
You've been in a fix
At the paper we have distributed.
We printed the plate
Meant for Class 8.
The typist has been executed.'

What happened to Zin?
In that kind loony bin
I'm sorry to say that they locked her

She sits there now
A quiet old frau
Supervised by a medical doctor.

For many a day
She has squatted that way
Serene as an egg newly laid.
Zinny's quite calm
The only alarm,
Should the doctor say, 'Tests to be made.'

Then old Zenobia
Shows off her phobia
Of the test, the quiz, the exams
Just a stool sample
Gives her an ample
Opportunity for the jimjams.

So if you're the kind
Of vomitous mind
That says she is going to fail
And quietly goes
And scores in crores
Remember Zenobia's tale.

This Is What Happens to Children Who Scream in Public

Little kids who scream and

Are likely to attract a clout.

This Is What Happens to Children Who Boast Incessantly

Jeronimo John, amazing twit,
Jeronimo John, stupid as spit,
Jeronimo John, whose mighty tongue
Could spew forth kilograms of dung.
Jeronimo John liked to boast
So much he was voted 'Kid Who's Most
Likely to Rise Early to Brag'
'My mother's divine.' (That old bag?)
'My father's double oh nine.' (He's a drag.)
'I write so well.' (Little liar.)
'I run so fast.' (With pants on fire…)
Jeronimo John couldn't see
How bored we were of his lying spree.

Jeronimo John, total bore
Once trundled off to Ranthambhore.
Even in the jungle, couldn't stop talking
Oblivious to the tiger stalking.

Did the langur not warn them all?
It did but who could hear its call?
Jeronimo John, tongue on 'roids,
He whom quietness avoids,
Overpowered every sound
For several hectares around.
The guide went white about the lips,
For the tourists would give him no tips,
If they didn't see the fabled cat
Which, after all, was the reason that
They had come to Ranthambhore.
The guide thought about it some more
And decided he would allow
The boy to descend at Padam Talao
For had not the little idiot said,
'With one arm tied to my bed
I can wrestle any old tiger
From Rajasthan to deepest Niger.'
Jeronimo John was on the spot
Jeronimo John was nicely caught
In a trap of which he was the maker
If he didn't get down, they'd call him faker.
Jeronimo John got off the Cantor
Jeronimo John started to banter

With those watching this incredible feat
(It was a performance, hard to beat.)
When out of the grass that rimmed the lake
Jumped a tiger, a cat on the make
Cat with four hungry mouths to feed
Cat whose hunting the tourists impede
Cat who hadn't eaten a bite
For half that day and at least a night.
Cat who now stretched its jaws
Cat who now unfurled its paws
To let the sun shine on its claws
Cat who admits no human laws
Cat who makes one swift bite
Cat who causes death by fright
Cat who now sits down to yawn
And spit up bits of Jeronimo John.

Of course, the guide was a little shocked
But then the whole Cantor was rocked
When all the tourists began to clap.
'I must say, you're quite a fine chap,'
'I must say, you're quite a brick.'
'You must explain how you work that trick.'
They showed no sign of decent sorrow.

'Can we do it again tomorrow?'
They asked thinking it was a lark
Set up by a canny national park,
A trick in which a fat young boy
Is fed to some tiger-like toy.
Not one of them did guess
That Jeronimo John was a mess
Of bone and gristle and hair and nails
Falling from under some tiger tails.

For half a moment let us mourn
The untimely death of Jeronimo John.
But if there's a lesson to be had
From the passing of the lad:
Even if you feel the pressing need
To boast about your simplest deed
Think how yucky you'd feel
Should you end up as a mid-day meal.

Camels

Camels
Are
Mammals
Even
Lazy
Slow lorises are, you know?

Bats

Bats scare me

All night long.

They might bite through my

Sarong.

Sad

It's okay to feel sad
(from time to time)
It's okay to feel blue
(It's not a crime).

Why not have a little cry?
(Cuddled up in bed)
Or let go and really bawl
(fit to wake the dead)?

It works for me
(And I'm quite old)
It will for you
(So I've been told).

Happy

Jump (quick!)
Puppy lick
Ice cream stick.

Hopscotch
Butterscotch
Rain splotch!

No school.
Swimming pool.
Toffee? Cool!

You and me
Shady tree
Two swings free!

Seasons

The spring is hot.
The summer is hot.

The monsoon is hot.
The winter is not.

Not very hot.
Just somewhat.

A Questoon

Hang a question from a string,
Under a blue moon.
Now you have a magic thing:
Your personal question.

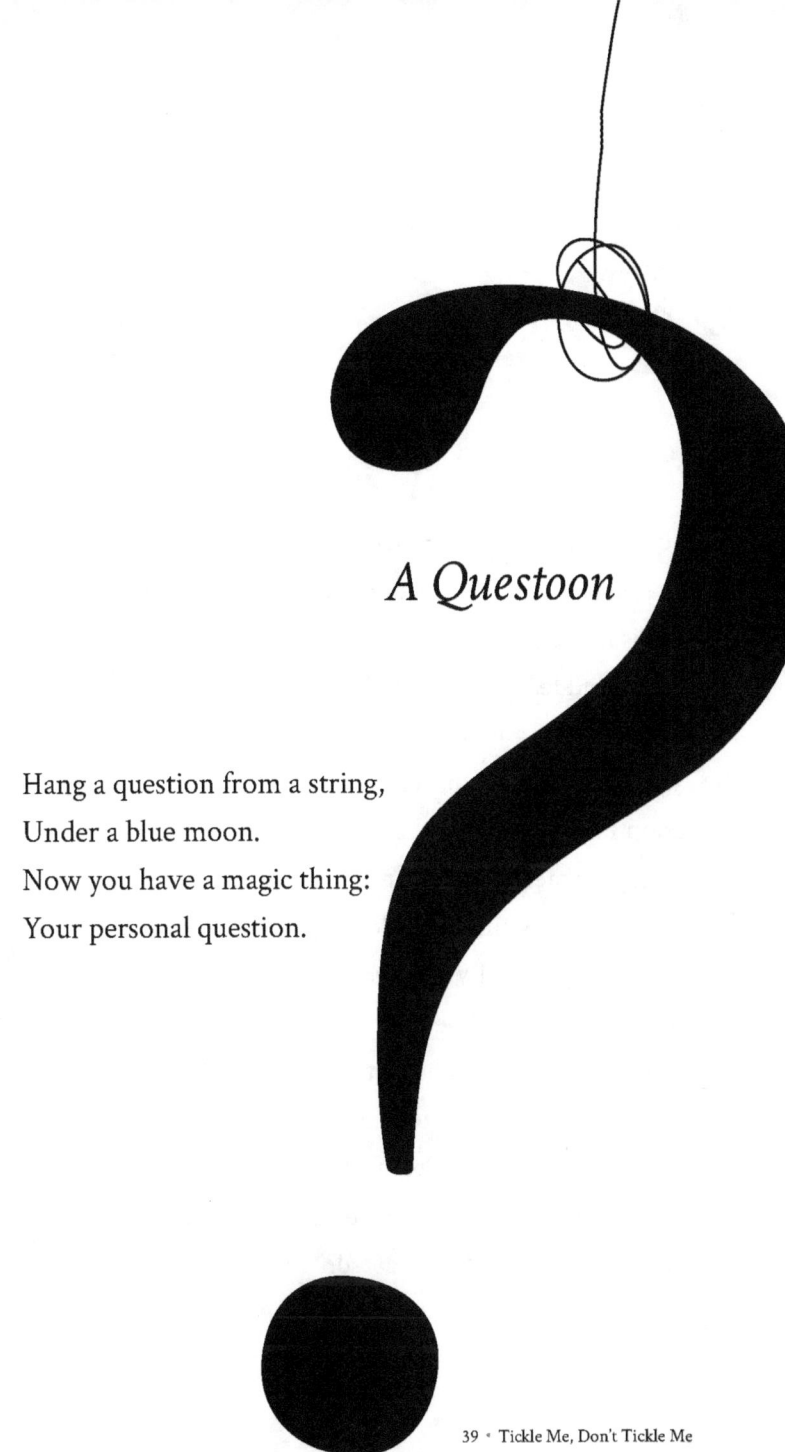

Loop D'Whoop and Champ

Loop D'Whoop, he gnawed a button,
Dreamed some dreams of chawing mutton.
In his larder, a cucumber,
Roots and leaves? You couldn't number!
Nothing that a wolf would eat
When his tummy lusts for meat.
Loop said, 'I am just what I am.
I long for meat, I long for lamb.
Had I my claws inside a bleater,
How completely I would eat her.
Not a sliver would be wasted.
Every morsel would be tasted.
And then I think this toothsome creature
In a cookbook might just feature.
Braised and boiled and stewed and roasted…
Can any bit of goat be toasted?'

Loop began to cast about
Saliva dripping from his snout.
In his head, he weighed each one
Soot and Snowy, Champ and Bun.
All the kids of Ms Caprine
(Of goat mothers, quite the queen)
A mum who fed her lambs each day
On heaps of clover-scented hay.

Looking at these kids at play,
Loop was often wont to say:
'Each one would make a three-course meal.
I'll just take one so she won't feel
Too bad or sad or mad about it.
Miss one kid? I rather doubt it.'

That evening at the close of day,
As all the young ones were at play,
Loop D'Whoop went to the park
And in his head he made a mark
On the succulent hindquarters
Of one of Ms Caprine's young daughters.

Ms Champ was the runt of the litter.
She never let this make her bitter.
Instead she worked a little harder
Ate all the food in her mum's larder
Ran some more and played for longer
Tried each day to become stronger.
Said Ms Caprine, 'Don't go by size.
There's a fire in her eyes.'

Loop D'Whoop now made a plan
He got himself a big fat can
Of sweetly-scented four-leaf clover,
Opened it and wandered over
To the spot where Champ was playing,
Showed her some of it while saying:
'Clover helps you dance and caper,
Found that in the best newspaper.'

Champ was quite a nosy coot
She'd sniff at shoe or sock or boot.
She'd check out a pile of rags.
She'd poke about at plastic bags.
When she was born, she didn't stop
To get a snack at Mom's Milk Shop.
Instead she tottered off to look
At the flapping pages of a book.

Champ was also very bright,
She knew that something wasn't right.
The can was full to overflowing.
Loop's eyes were also strangely glowing.
'Look kid,' Loop said, 'It's not like that.
Would I eat Ms Caprine's brat?
Or think of ways to cook your meat?
When there's almost zilch to eat?'

'Your eyes are shining rather brightly.'
'Oh don't be silly,' Loop said lightly.
'If you find this to your taste.
I'll throw in free wasabi paste.'

Free! The world reeled and hopped.
Free! Champ's heart clipped and clopped.
Like any other Indian girl,
'Free' really made her senses swirl.
(Yes, the word is quite a joy,
Even to the Indian boy.
I simply put in 'girl' at that time,
Because I had to find a rhyme.)

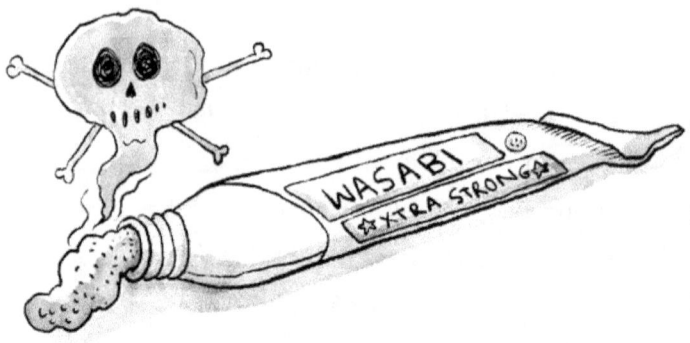

Champ said, 'May I see the box?'
Loop pulled one out from his socks.
Champ slipped the box behind her ear.
'Done deal?' Loop asked. 'Now you come here.'
He led her to a shady glade,
Where he'd concealed a shiny blade
With which to skin her, skull to trotter.
(He was a very hungry rotter.)

Champ began to chomp the hay
When Loop gave his fell game away.
He flashed out his shiny sharpsome knife
'This is the end of your short life.
Oh don't you weep, oh don't you cry.
You're off to gambol in the sky.'

Champ thought quickly and then said,
'Very soon I'll end up dead.
I would hate so much to waste
This fine and super-tasty paste.
If you'd let me, my fine friend,
I'll smear myself from end to end.
That way you'll have a finer meal.
Now may I break this box's seal?'

'Well,' said Loop. 'That is quite wise
No tears? No pleas? No plaintive cries?
Yes, I think that you could do
With some green and piquant goo.'

Champ dug out a nice big glob.
And threw it into Loop's fat gob.
It hit his nose; it hit his eyes.
All the forest heard his cries.
Wasabi may look cool and green.
But in your eyes? It's very mean.

'Oh Loopy, are your eyes aflame?
You only have yourself to blame.'
Champ then took poor Loopy back
To Dr (Mrs) Bigwigsack.
She prescribed some cooling lotions.
Also pills and bitter potions.
After several weeks had passed
Loopy's eyes were fine at last.
But they never looked again
At kid or pigling, quail or hen.

Cootie at the Baker's

At the bakery, Cootie said,
'Give me a bun that has bread.'

    The baker said, 'Son, if you please,
    That will cost you no rupees.'

Cootie scratched his head and bum,
'It'll take a while to save that sum.'

    The baker said, 'I cannot wait
    Come back soon, it might get late.'

Cootie said with a look forlorn
'I can't return before I'm gone.'

History (in brief)

Some king, somewhere, he felt cheated.
He attacked, an army retreated.
That left the other king unseated.
People died, food stocks depleted.
You would think we'd all get wiser,
Prince and PM, king and kaiser.
But the nations (all the big ones)
Go on making bombs and big guns.

True Story

Sir Hans Sloane was a collecting fellow
He picked up a snake that was rather yellow.
Most people would think that quite enough
But Sir Hans was made of British stuff:
He trained it to follow at his heel!
But perhaps a seven-foot snake might feel
A bit off-colour at this poodlesome plight,
So he escaped at the dead of night.
This happened on board a ship from Jamaica.

Among the sailors, not a hostage taker.
Boom! Bang! went their guns, Kaboom! Kersplat!
They killed that poor reptile just like that.
Poor Sir Sloane was rather blue.
He said, 'I have other animals too.'
The Captain coughed and turned aside.
The steward said, 'Your iguana died!'
'What's happening to my animal hoard?'
'Oh, Iggy simply jumped overboard.'
And before they docked the ship at Dover
Sloane's alligator's life was over.
Poor Sir Hans, he sure could lose 'em
So he set up the British Museum.

PS: This did happen. Sir Hans Sloane (1660–1753) went to Jamaica and brought back a huge treasure trove of things and a yellow snake which he trained to walk behind him, an iguana and an alligator. They died on board the ship as I have described above but perhaps the iguana swam home. This was the only trip Sir Hans Sloane made abroad but he collected so many things that when he died, his collections formed the basis of the British Museum.

In Defence of Rudy

*Poor Rudyard Kipling was frightened by a Bombay hen
and his father, J. Lockwood Kipling, wrote
a rather rude limerick about it.*

There was a small boy of Bombay
Who once from a hen ran away
They said, 'You're a baby.'
He said, 'Maybe.
But I don't like those hens of Bombay.'

> *One day, I was coming home and there was a rat
> on the stairs. A huge rat and it was coming down
> the stairs. I went quickly out of the building
> and waited until it had made a stately exit.
> And so I wrote a poem:*

Much time has passed since the day when
Young Rudy was scared by a Bombay hen.
J. Lockwood, come to a Bombay flat
And try to face down a Bombay rat.

Zoo Announcement

Our Slow Stochastic Indicator*
Escaped from her cage at the zoo.
We hope she will be captured later
Or else there will be a to-do.

Our Slow Stochastic Indicator
Is happy to dine on her meat.
At the zoo, we feed her alligator
And a jug of buttermilk neat.

If a Slow Stochastic Indicator
Looks at you in the bus
Try to look like a dried-up potato
Or carry your old arquebus.

---

* A Stochastic Indicator is a term in economics which is supposed to help you understand when to trade stocks. I just thought it would make a great name for an animal specially since it is also sometimes called the Slow Stochastic Oscillator.

But a Slow Stochastic Indicator
Will never be easy to fool
You'd better not rile or incite her
Or you'll pretty much end up as stool.

Our Slow Stochastic Indicator
Is quiet and quick on her feet
Wildlife groups want to aid and abet her
Escape to a stock-broker's sheet.

The Hamster

Beware the hamster.
Such a scamster.
Under his fur, there's not a gram
Of any shape or form of ham.

Question

Inside a **turkey** Is there a bull

Yes, you would
find one for certain
In Istanbul.

Hungry in Mathematics Class

I don't know the value of π
But a pizza costs fifty rupees.
The graphs that I draw run awry
All I want is a pie chart with cheese.

A Mathematical Love Story

I once knew a helix Whose name was Felix. He wed a svelte hyperbola Her friends were wont to call her Yola.

They had a baby:
A sine-curve maybe?

For details, send faxes
To the z-axis.

My Cat

'Fat cat
On the mat
Look at that
Dirty rat.'

                    'That rat
                    is rather fat.
                    for that matter
                    it's even fatter
                    than I.
                    So why
                    don't you try
                    To catch that rat
                    While I sit on my mat?'

Our Puppy

We took him home, we called him Cuddles.
Pa says we better call him Puddles.

Which Puppy?

It doesn't matter which pup one picks
One end wiggles, the other end
licks.

Puppy Licks

I thought I'd give my puppy an ellum,
>right on his smellum.

I shouldn't have told Ma.
>How she was yellum.

>>Ma: Do you suppose
>>His nose
>>is a rose?

She said I might fall illum.
I told my puppy
So my puppy gave me an ellum,
>On my smellum.

More Ink!

My pen is full of inky-ink.
I'm going to have a thinky-think
If I think up something bright.
I'll sit me down and writey-write.
But I may need more ink because
So much ends up on my paws.

Sellin' a Melon

What are you sellin'?

          A melon.

What sort of melon?

          Water melon.

What a melon!

          That's what I'm sellin'

Why you yellin'?

          When you're sellin'
          A melon
          You gotta be yellin'.

Kiwi, Kiwi, Kiwikiwi

Even Cootie the galoot
Knows the kiwi is a fruit.

And you, my learned friend, have heard
The kiwi is a flightless bird.

Perhaps it might shock you to learn
The kiwikiwi is a pretty fern.

I'd Rather Read

Some like to garden and happily weed;
I'd rather read.
Some like to run till their feet bleed;
I'd rather read.
Some chop and fry and churn and knead;
I'd rather read.
Some like to study. (Indeed? Indeed!)
I'd rather read.

Now I've brought you up to speed:
Others may do; I'd rather read.
So don't you beg and don't you plead.
I won't play in the team you lead.
I'm not the eleventh man you need.
I'd rather read.

Peppy of the Steppe

Out in the middle of the darkling steppe,
Lived a woman who was totally

Pep

She had no money, she had no land.
But still she believed that life was grand.
She smiled so much, she split her face
And sewed it up and added lace.
She laughed and laughed and split her sides
And let you look at her insides.

If you asked her why she laughed a lot
She said, 'Oh come, it's really not
So tough to smile when you have kids.
They show you life is not on skids.
When things look grim, when I want to frown.
One of them begins to clown.
I feel a smile begin to wriggle
Along my lips. And then I giggle.
Things can never be so bad.
As long as a laugh is to be had.'

Her children were a happy bunch.
There were six who sat with her for lunch.
There never was too much to eat.
But by a strange and magic feat.
Their mother put food upon the table.
She worked as hard as she was able.

Peppy, that was her given name,
She tried to teach her kids the same
Things she had learned from her Mum.
How to stitch and spin and hum.
How to love all living forms
How to live by nature's norms.

When one wanted to kill a bat,
She asked, 'What do you think you're at?'
When one of them pursued a kitten,
She gave him what for with a mitten.
Once she saved a shivering spider
That fell into a glass of cider.
Peppy was that kind of person.
You felt warm without your furs on.

But you can bet it's never easy
To be poor when it gets freezy.
November brought with it snow flurries
December brought its share of worries.
Christmas, what a time of year!
But money helps to make good cheer.
You've got to bake a Christmas cake
And you've got gifts that you must make.
You must find a Christmas tree.
Nothing ever comes for free.

Peppy—a far-thinking creature—
Her garden's most important feature
Was a conifer she had planted
When the earth was slightly slanted
Athwart the sun when it was spring.
(That's a ge-o-graphy thing.)

So she had a Christmas tree,
Ready, fine and green and free.
Now she needed bric a brac
Stars and spangles, (some blue tack?)
To make the tree look tippy-top
To make her children dance and hop.

But stars and fairies, gosh and golly
Cost a fair amount of lolly.
Smiles she had. Laughs? Oh so many.
But as for money, she hadn't any.
'It would be nice if that pine tree,
Were all decked up for the kids to see.'
So she sighed and went to bed.
Tired, she slumbered like the dead.

Outside the house, a shivery spider,
(The one Peppy rescued from the cider?)
Spun her silk from twig to twig
She almost gave that tree a wig.
When she was done, a scatter of rain
Left water shining on the main
Bits of the web and then those froze.
When in the morning the children rose,
They screamed with great delight to see
A shiny sparkly Christmas tree.

The weak and watery winter sun
Illuminated every one
Of the spicules that were shining
With a fine and icy lining.

Peppy smiled to see her tree.
Said she, 'The best things in life are free.'

Stubby Joe

Inkus Pinkus,
My big toe,
Why d'you always hurt me so?

Inkus Pinkus,
My big toe,
I'm going to call you Stubby Joe.

> Stinkus Finkus, it's
> Stubby Joe.
> I'm your friend and not your foe.
> Why don't *you* look where you go?

Tickle Me, Don't Tickle Me

Tickle me, don't tickle me.
What can I say? I'm fickle me.
I want to giggle, I want to laugh.
But too much tickling and I'll barf.
I've eaten lots this morning so
It might come out, all gluggety go.
Tickle me, tickle me, go on then.
I want to go and eat again.

Breakfast Rhymes

Oh yay,
It's pohé.

Nothing fiddly,
Just an idli.

Put some butter
On my aloo mutter.

Oh sir, oh sir,
Make mine a dosa.

No dosa?
Then a samosa.

No samosa? What a hum!
Please mine an uttappam.

At the most,
Buttered toast.

Can I please
Have some cheese?

Oh well then, maybe
Milk and jilebi.

I feel grungy
If I don't have kanji.

Reading

The more you read, the more you know.
The more you know, the more you grow.
The more you grow, the more you live.
The more you live, the more you give.
The more you give, the more you get.
Nothing outdoes reading yet!

Girly

Girly, girly, whose hairs are curly,
In this mad-mad hurly-burly
All I see is a 'copter twirly
Lost in your mop, curly girly.

Girly, girly, your tooths are pearly
Perhaps you get up early early
Toothpaste getting full unfairly
Brushing brushing ruhlly-ruhlly

Girly, girly, don't be surly.
Whyfor are you so churly?
Let me tell you, you're not Shirley.
Your chachi doesn't live in Worli.

Hair-oil Horror

It must take an awful lot of toil
To make a pint of coconut oil.
It must make oil-press men see red
When Mama pours it on my head.

I wouldn't mind much if it would
Stay where it might do some good
But what I think is a disgrace
Is how it slithers down my face.

It makes me look a silly goose
Ma says, 'Just pretend it's mousse.'
'Yeah, right, Ma,' I want to quip.
'It's just that mousses do not drip.'

Ma says, 'But you'll have lovely hair!'
To which I say, 'I have to bear
Them laughing when the oil is found
Running off me to the ground.'

I'm sure if oily kids were called
We'd all vote to end up bald.
We wouldn't have to bear the scorn
Of oily hair if we were shorn.

But nothing we can do will foil
Our mothers' love of coc'nut oil.

Advice to Mothers

A cup of milk
goes down like silk.
If you put in it
a bit
of chocolate.

There's a Monster in My Garden

Inspector James, I beg your pardon,
There's a monster in my garden.

What a bother, what irritation!
That's a job for the fire station!

Mr Fireman, beg your pardon,
There's a monster in my garden

Oh that's sad, just call me Gordon.
Now go and tell the forest warden.

Mr Warden, beg your pardon,
There's a monster in my garden.

I can't leave my post, I daren't.
That's a job for someone's parent.

But don't you see, I beg your pardon.
It's *my* mother in the garden.

They Took Papa Away in a Car

They took Papa away in a car
They took him at four in the morning.
They've taken him somewhere far
Where the words don't rhyme
Because everything gets stuck in my throat.

And I want to cry but I can't.
Nani does all the crying.
Ma doesn't cry.
She pulls her lips into her face
And goes to court.
I don't ask to go with her.

I don't ask because I asked Nani once,
'Why did they take Papa?'
And she said, 'Do you want to kill me, beta?'
I don't want to kill Nani.
I only want to know where Papa is.
Left-side aunty said, 'Good children don't ask questions.'
Right-side aunty said, 'Did he think he was going to
      save the world?'

So I don't ask questions.
And I swallow hard.
And wait for the time
The words will start rhyming again.

Whatever the Weather

Day before yesterday, it was cloudy.
I opened my window and thanked the clouds.
They bring rain and the rain makes things grow.

Yesterday, it was raining.
I opened my window and thanked the rain.
If it rains enough, they may cancel school.

Yesterday, it was sunny.
I opened my window and thanked the sun.
The sun gives us heat and light and it's all free.

I don't know what the weather will be like tomorrow
But I'm ready.
I'm going to smile at the weather, whatever it's like.
And look, I'm going to

s m i l e

at you.

I'm smiling. I'm smiling.

And look you're smiling back.

It's catching. Look, she's smiling too. And she's smiling.

We're all smiling.

I think the world's already a better place.

I'm going but YOU,

YOU

Keep that smile going.

When the Music Starts

When the music starts
Just get up and dance
No no-es, no can't's
Just get up and dance.
Just get up and dance
Dance-dance, dance dance.

Jump, jump about, jump, jiggle and prance
Who's looking at you? There's not one glance!
They're dancing to glory.
They're taking their chance,
To get up and dance
To get up and dance.
Dance-dance, dance, dance,
Dance-dance, dance dance.

Grab your parents, your uncles and aunts,
If they won't come, just get up and dance.
This isn't an evening of ballet in France.
Just get up and dance.
Just get up and dance.

When the Music Stops

When the music stops
And it generally does
Don't stop those hops
Just keep the buzz.

Let the music play
In your radiohead
Take the beats away
To school, to bed.

Let it thump, let it bump
In your legs, in your hands.
When the music stops,
Do your own lungi dance.

What Do You Want to Be When You Grow Up?

I'll drive a taxi
In Cotopaxi.

        I'll cure disease
        With the greatest of ease.

I'll dance with joy
At the Russian Bolshoi.

        I'll win a Grammy,
        And say, 'That's for Mammy.'

I'll have close shaves,
When I explore caves.

> I'll go to live with Chandu Mama
> And become a cabbage farmer.

I'll study with Eklavya Chacha
And become an Olympic Archer.

> I'll be a book-binder
> Or a great organ-grinder;
> I'll be a child-minder
> Or a criminal-finder.

I'll be a watch-maker
Or a lone census-taker.
I'll be a cake baker
Or a verdant lawn-raker.

> I don't know yet what I want to do.
> But whatever I do, what's it to you?
> I'll have you know I'm only ten
> Who knows what I will want when
> I'm twenty or thirty or even forty?
> I might be nice, I might be naughty.

I might be a banker
I might drive a tanker
Lower an anchor
Or cut off a canker.

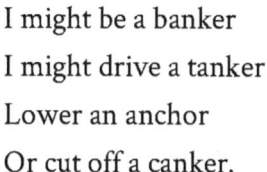

Whatever I'll be, let me tell you chappy,
I plan to be ext-urr-emely happy.

Whatever I'll be,
I will be me

Jerry Pinto *lives in a city.*
This is a pity
Because cities ain't pretty.
Jerry Pinto writes
And won't fly kites.
Kites hurt birds and birds have rights.
Jerry Pinto is old
His knees won't fold
When the weather is cold.
But Jerry's tongue
is still young.
(Ching chung.)
What is Ching Chung?
That is a bell.
It says: Nothing else is going to rhyme.
Not this time.